This record book belongs to

MW01154140

School _____   Phone _____

Grade _____   Room _____   Year _____

Contents

Record student names across the top.

Record dates of assessments or use a section for each quarter of the year.

Record individual proficiencies at each date. You may choose to use any system, such as check marks, a 1–4 rubric, letters, or grades.

Cara Avery				Luis Diaz				Sam Edwards				Jay	
9/6	9/8	10/15	2/3	9/6	9/8	10/15	2/3	9/6	9/8	10/15	2/3	9/6	9/
1	1	2	2	3	3	3	4	1	2	2	3	2	3
- struggles with counting objects and counting on fingers				- understands concepts of addition and subtraction				- successful with verbal explanations				- strugg subtra	

K.OA.A.1

Add detailed notes throughout the year.

For a more comprehensive resource guide with tips and additional reproducibles, visit *activities.carsondellosa.com*.

ISBN 978-1-4838-1111-6
01-135147784

Math Standards At a Glance

Know the number names and the count sequence.

K.CC.A.1 Count to 100 by ones and by tens.

K.CC.A.2 Count forward beginning from a given number within the known sequence (instead of having to begin at 1).

K.CC.A.3 Write numbers from 0 to 20. Represent a number of objects with a written numeral 0–20 (with 0 representing a count of no objects).

Count to tell the number of objects.

K.CC.B.4 Understand the relationship between numbers and quantities; connect counting to cardinality.

> **K.CC.B.4a** When counting objects, say the number names in the standard order, pairing each object with one and only one number name and each number name with one and only one object.
>
> **K.CC.B.4b** Understand that the last number name said tells the number of objects counted. The number of objects is the same regardless of their arrangement or the order in which they were counted.
>
> **K.CC.B.4c** Understand that each successive number name refers to a quantity that is one larger.

K.CC.B.5 Count to answer "how many?" questions about as many as 20 things arranged in a line, a rectangular array, or a circle, or as many as 10 things in a scattered configuration; given a number from 1–20, count out that many objects.

Compare Numbers

K.CC.C.6 Identify whether the number of objects in one group is greater than, less than, or equal to the number of objects in another group.

K.CC.C.7 Compare two numbers between 1 and 10 presented as written numerals.

Understand addition as putting together and adding to, and understanding subtraction as taking apart and taking from.

K.OA.A.1 Represent addition and subtraction with objects, fingers, mental images, drawings, sounds , acting out situations, verbal explanations, expressions, or equations.

K.OA.A.2 Solve addition and subtraction word problems, and add and subtract within 10.

K.OA.A.3 Decompose numbers less than or equal to 10 into pairs in more than one way and record each decomposition by a drawing or equation.

K.OA.A.4 For any number from 1 to 9, find the number that makes 10 when added to the given number and record the answer with a drawing or equation.

K.OA.A.5 Fluently add and subtract within 5.

Work with numbers 11–19 to gain foundations for place value.

K.NBT.A.1 Compose and decompose numbers from 11 to 19 into ten ones and some further ones and record each composition or decomposition by a drawing or equation; understand that these numbers are composed of ten ones and one, two, three, four, five, six, seven, eight, or nine ones.

Describe and compare measurable attributes.

K.MD.A.1 Describe measurable attributes of objects, such as length or weight. Describe several measurable attributes of a single object.

K.MD.A.2 Directly compare two objects with a measurable attribute in common, to see which object has "more of"/"less of" the attribute, and describe the difference.

Classify objects and count the number of objects in each category.

K.MD.B.3 Classify objects into given categories; count the numbers of objects in each category and sort the categories by count.

Identify and describe shapes (squares, circles, triangles, rectangles, hexagons, cubes, cones, cylinders, and spheres).

K.G.A.1 Describe objects in the environment using names of shapes, and describe the relative positions of these objects using terms such as *above*, *below*, *beside*, *in front of*, *behind*, and *next to*.

K.G.A.2 Correctly name shapes regardless of their orientations or overall size.

K.G.A.3 Identify shapes as two-dimensional (lying in a plane, "flat" or three-dimensional "solid").

Analyze, compare, create, and compose shapes.

K.G.B.4 Analyze and compare two- and three-dimensional shapes, in different sizes and orientations, using informal language to describe their similarities, differences, parts and other attributes.

K.G.B.5 Model shapes in the world by building shapes from components and drawing shapes.

K.G.B.6 Compose simple shapes to form larger shapes.

Language Arts Standards At a Glance

RL

Key Ideas and Details

RL.K.1 With prompting and support, ask and answer questions about key details in a text.

RL.K.2 With prompting and support, retell familiar stories, including key details.

RL.K.3 With prompting and support, identify characters, settings, and major events in a story.

Craft and Structure

RL.K.4 Ask and answer questions about unknown words in a text.

RL.K.5 Recognize common types of texts.

RL.K.6 With prompting and support, name the author and illustrator of a story and define the role of each in telling the story.

Integration of Knowledge and Ideas

RL.K.7 With prompting and support, describe the relationship between illustrations and the story in which they appear.

RL.K.8 (not applicable to literature)

RL.K.9 With prompting and support, compare and contrast the adventures and experiences of characters in familiar stories.

Range of Reading and Level of Text Complexity

RL.K.10 Actively engage in group reading activities with purpose and understanding.

RI

Key Ideas and Details

RI.K.1 With prompting and support, ask and answer questions about key details in a text.

RI.K.2 With prompting and support, identify the main topic and retell key details of a text.

RI.K.3 With prompting and support, describe the connection between two individuals, events, ideas, or pieces of information in a text.

Craft and Structure

RI.K.4 With prompting and support, ask and answer questions about unknown words in a text.

RI.K.5 Identify the front cover, back cover, and title page of a book.

RI.K.6 Name the author and illustrator of a text and define the role of each in presenting the ideas or information in a text.

Integration of Knowledge and Ideas

RI.K.7 With prompting and support, describe the relationship between illustrations and the text in which they appear.

RI.K.8 With prompting and support, identify the reasons an author gives to support points in a text.

RI.K.9 With prompting and support, identify basic similarities in and differences between two texts on the same topic.

Range of Reading and Level of Text Complexity

RI.K.10 Actively engage in group reading activities with purpose and understanding.

RF

Print Concepts

RF.K.1 Demonstrate understanding of the organization and basic features of print.

  RF.K.1a Follow words from left to right, top to bottom, and page by page.

  RF.K.1b Recognize that spoken words are represented in written language by specific sequences of letters.

  RF.K.1c Understand that words are separated by spaces in print.

  RF.K.1d Recognize and name all upper- and lowercase letters of the alphabet.

Phonological Awareness

RF.K.2 Demonstrate understanding of spoken words, syllables, and sounds (phonemes).

  RF.K.2a Recognize and produce rhyming words.

  RF.K.2b Count, pronounce, blend, and segment syllables in spoken words.

  RF.K.2c Blend and segment onsets and rimes of single-syllable spoken words.

  RF.K.2d Isolate and pronounce the initial, medial vowel, and final sounds (phonemes) in three-phoneme (consonant-vowel-consonant, or CVC) words. (This does not include CVCs ending with /l/, /r/, or /x/.)

  RF.K.2e Add or substitute individual sounds (phonemes) in simple, one-syllable words to make new words.

Phonics and Word Recognition

RF.K.3 Know and apply grade-level phonics and word analysis skills in decoding words.

  RF.K.3a Demonstrate basic knowledge of one-to-one letter-sound correspondences by producing the primary sound or many of the most frequent sounds for each consonant.

  RF.K.3b Associate the long and short sounds with the common spellings (graphemes) for the five major vowels.

  RF.K.3c Read common high-frequency words by sight.

  RF.K.3d Distinguish between similarly spelled words by identifying the sounds of the letters that differ.

Fluency

RF.K.4 Read emergent-reader texts with purpose and understanding.

Text Types and Purposes

W.K.1 Use a combination of drawing, dictating, and writing to compose opinion pieces in which they tell a reader the topic or the name of the book they are writing about and state an opinion or preference about the topic or book.

W.K.2 Use a combination of drawing, dictating, and writing to compose informative/explanatory texts in which they name what they are writing about and supply some information about the topic.

W.K.3 Use a combination of drawing, dictating, and writing to narrate a single event or several loosely linked events, tell about the events in the order in which they occurred, and provide a reaction to what happened.

Production and Distribution of Writing

W.K.4 (begins in grade 3)

W.K.5 With guidance and support from adults, respond to questions and suggestions from peers and add details to strengthen writing as needed.

W.K.6 With guidance and support from adults, explore a variety of digital tools to produce and publish writing, including in collaboration with peers.

Research to Build and Present Knowledge

W.K.7 Participate in shared research and writing projects.

W.K.8 With guidance and support from adults, recall information from experiences or gather information from provided sources to answer a question.

W.K.9 (begins in grade 4)

Range of Writing

W.K.10 (begins in grade 3)

Comprehension and Collaboration

SL.K.1 Participate in collaborative conversations with diverse partners about *kindergarten topics and texts* with peers and adults in small and larger groups.

  SL.K.1a Follow agreed-upon rules for discussions.

  SL.K.1b Continue a conversation through multiple exchanges.

SL.K.2 Confirm understanding of a text read aloud or information presented orally or through other media by asking and answering questions about key details and requesting clarification if something is not understood.

SL.K.3 Ask and answer questions in order to seek help, get information, or clarify something that is not understood.

Presentation of Knowledge and Ideas

SL.K.4 Describe familiar people, places, things, and events and, with prompting and support, provide additional detail.

SL.K.5 Add drawings or other visual displays to descriptions as desired to provide additional detail.

SL.K.6 Speak audibly and express thoughts, feelings, and ideas clearly.

Conventions of Standard English

L.K.1 Demonstrate command of the conventions of standard English grammar and usage when writing or speaking.

  L.K.1a Print many upper- and lowercase letters.

  L.K.1b Use frequently occurring nouns and verbs.

  L.K.1c Form regular plural nouns orally by adding /s/ or /es/.

  L.K.1d Understand and use question words (interrogatives).

  L.K.1e Use the most frequently occurring prepositions.

  L.K.1f Produce and expand complete sentences in shared language activities.

L.K.2 Demonstrate command of the conventions of standard English capitalization, punctuation, and spelling when writing.

  L.K.2a Capitalize the first word in a sentence and the pronoun *I*.

  L.K.2b Recognize and name end punctuation.

  L.K.2c Write a letter or letters for most consonant and short-vowel sounds (phonemes).

  L.K.2d Spell simple words phonetically, drawing on knowledge of sound-letter relationships.

Knowledge of Language

L.K.3 (begins in grade 2)

Vocabulary Acquisition and Use

L.K.4 Determine or clarify the meaning of unknown and multiple-meaning words and phrases based on kindergarten reading and content.

  L.K.4a Identify new meanings for familiar words and apply them accurately.

  L.K.4b Use the most frequently occurring inflections and affixes as a clue to the meaning of an unknown word.

L.K.5 With guidance and support from adults, explore word relationships and nuances in word meanings.

  L.K.5a Sort common objects into categories to gain a sense of the concepts the categories represent.

  L.K.5b Demonstrate understanding of frequently occurring verbs and adjectives by relating them to their opposites (antonyms).

  L.K.5c Identify real-life connections between words and their use.

  L.K.5d Distinguish shades of meaning among verbs describing the same general action by acting out the meanings.

L.K.6 Use words and phrases acquired through conversations, reading and being read to, and responding to texts.

Counting and Cardinality

K.CC.A.1

Count to 100 by ones and by tens.

K.CC.A.2

Count forward beginning from a given number within the known sequence (instead of having to begin at 1).

K.CC.A.3

Write numbers from 0 to 20. Represent a number of objects with a written numeral 0–20 (with 0 representing a count of no objects).

K.CC.B.4

Understand the relationship between numbers and quantities; connect counting to cardinality.
  K.CC.B.4a When counting objects, say the number names in the standard order, pairing each object with one and only one number name and each number name with one and only one object.
  K.CC.B.4b Understand that the last number name said tells the number of objects counted. The number of objects is the same regardless of their arrangement or the order in which they were counted.
  K.CC.B.4c Understand that each successive number name refers to a quantity that is one larger.

K.CC.B.5

Count to answer "how many?" questions about as many as 20 things arranged in a line, a rectangular array, or a circle, or as many as 10 things in a scattered configuration; given a number from 1–20, count out that many objects.

K.CC.C.6

Identify whether the number of objects in one group is greater than, less than, or equal to the number of objects in another group, e.g., by using matching and counting strategies.
(Include groups with up to ten objects.)

K.CC.C.7

Compare two numbers between 1 and 10 presented as written numerals.

_____

_____

_____

_____

_____

Standards Crosswalk

Prekindergarten*

Children should demonstrate increasing competency in the following, with guidance and support:

- Count up to 10 objects using one-to-one correspondence.
- Begin counting forward from a given number in a known sequence.
- Without counting, identify the number of objects in a collection of up to five objects.
- In counting, understand the number name of the last object counted represents the total number of objects in the group.
- Recognize *first* and *last* as related to the order or position of objects.
- Determine, by counting or matching, if two sets (up to 10 objects) are equal, greater than, or less than.

First Grade

Number and Operations in Base Ten[†]

Extend the counting sequence.

- Read, write, count, and represent numbers from 0–120.

Understand place value.

- Compare two two-digit numbers using >, =, and <.

---

*Although Common Core State Standards are not yet available for prekindergarten, Pre-K students may be expected to demonstrate some level of competency for these skills.

[†]Counting and Cardinality is only a kindergarten domain.

K.CC.A.1																		
K.CC.A.2																		
K.CC.A.3																		
K.CC.B.4																		
K.CC.B.5																		
K.CC.C.6																		
K.CC.C.7																		

K.CC.A.1																				
K.CC.A.2																				
K.CC.A.3																				
K.CC.B.4																				
K.CC.B.5																				
K.CC.C.6																				
K.CC.C.7																				

K.CC.A.1																			
K.CC.A.2																			
K.CC.A.3																			
K.CC.B.4																			
K.CC.B.5																			
K.CC.C.6																			
K.CC.C.7																			

12

© Carson-Dellosa CD-104799

Operations and Algebraic Thinking

K.OA.A.1 Represent addition and subtraction with objects, fingers, mental images, drawings, sounds (e.g., claps), acting out situations, verbal explanations, expressions, or equations.

K.OA.A.2 Solve addition and subtraction word problems, and add and subtract within 10, e.g., by using objects or drawings to represent the problem.

K.OA.A.3 Decompose numbers less than or equal to 10 into pairs in more than one way, e.g., by using objects or drawings, and record each decomposition by a drawing or equation (e.g., $5 = 2 + 3$ and $5 = 4 + 1$).

K.OA.A.4 For any number from 1 to 9, find the number that makes 10 when added to the given number, e.g., by using objects or drawings, and record the answer with a drawing or equation.

K.OA.A.5 Fluently add and subtract within 5.

Standards Crosswalk

Prekindergarten*

Children should demonstrate increasing competency in the following, with guidance and support:

- Recognize there are more when sets of objects are combined.
- Recognize there are less when objects are removed.
- Use concrete objects (sums up to 10) to solve practical problems such as *If we have 2 apples and add 2 more, how many apples do we have altogether?*

First Grade

Operations and Algebraic Thinking

Represent and solve problems involving addition and subtraction.

- Use addition and subtraction within 20 to solve word problems with unknowns in all positions (including those represented by a symbol).
- Solve addition word problems with three numbers whose sum is less than or equal to 20.

Understand and apply properties of operations and the relationship between addition and subtraction.

- Apply properties of operations as strategies to add and subtract.
- Understand subtraction as an unknown-addend problem.

Add and subtract within 20.

- Relate counting to addition and subtraction.
- Use strategies to add and subtract within 20.
- Demonstrate fluency with addition and subtraction within 10.

Work with addition and subtraction equations.

- Understand the meaning of the equal sign.
- Determine if addition and subtraction equations are true or false.
- Find the unknown number in addition and subtraction equations.

*Although Common Core State Standards are not yet available for prekindergarten, Pre-K students may be expected to demonstrate some level of competency for these skills.

K.OA.A.1																			
K.OA.A.2																			
K.OA.A.3																			
K.OA.A.4																			
K.OA.A.5																			

16

K.OA.A.1																				
K.OA.A.2																				
K.OA.A.3																				
K.OA.A.4																				
K.OA.A.5																				

K.OA.A.1																				
K.OA.A.2																				
K.OA.A.3																				
K.OA.A.4																				
K.OA.A.5																				

20

Operations and Algebraic Thinking

© Carson-Dellosa CD-104799

21

Number and Operations in Base Ten

K.NBT.A.1

Compose and decompose numbers from 11 to 19 into ten ones and some further ones, e.g., by using objects or drawings, and record each composition or decomposition by a drawing or equation (such as 18 = 10 + 8); understand that these numbers are composed of ten ones and one, two, three, four, five, six, seven, eight, or nine ones.

Standards Crosswalk

Prekindergarten*

Children should demonstrate increasing competency in the following, with guidance and support:

- Recite numbers up to 20.
- Recognize and name numbers 1–10.
- Understand the relationship between numbers and quantities up to 10.
- Combine a concrete set of objects to equal a set no larger than 10.
- Remove a concrete set of objects from a set no larger than 10.

First Grade

Number and Operations in Base Ten

Extend the counting sequence.

- Read, write, count, and represent numbers within 120.

Understand place value.

- Understand that the digits of a two-digit number represent tens and ones.
- Understand that the numbers 11–19 are made of a 10 and a set of ones.
- Relate counting by 10s to place value.
- Compare two two-digit numbers using >, =, and < symbols.

Use place value understanding and properties of operations to add and subtract.

- Add within 100, including adding a two-digit and a one-digit number and adding multiples of tens to a two-digit number.
- Understand that in adding two-digit numbers, tens and tens are added, and ones and ones are added.
- Mentally find 10 more or 10 less than a given two-digit number.
- Subtract multiples of 10 in the range 10–90 from multiples of 10 in the same range.

*Although Common Core State Standards are not yet available for prekindergarten, Pre-K students may be expected to demonstrate some level of competency for these skills.

K.NBT.A.1

K.NBT.A.1

K.NBT.A.1

Measurement and Data

K.MD.A.1

Describe measurable attributes of objects, such as length or weight. Describe several measurable attributes of a single object.

K.MD.A.2

Directly compare two objects with a measurable attribute in common, to see which object has "more of"/"less of" the attribute, and describe the difference. *For example, directly compare the heights of two children and describe one child as taller/shorter.*

K.MD.B.3

Classify objects into given categories; count the numbers of objects in each category and sort the categories by count.
(Limit category counts to be less than or equal to 10.)

Standards Crosswalk

Prekindergarten*

Children should demonstrate increasing competency in the following, with guidance and support:

- Compare two objects by length, weight, or height directly by comparing objects side by side or indirectly using a third object.
- Use a unit of non-standard measurement to measure the length, weight, or height of one or more objects.
- Use measurement vocabulary and comparing terms such as *shorter*, *longer*, *lightest*, and *heaviest*.
- Classify, sort, and count a number of objects up to 10.
- Sort and classify objects by one or more attributes.
- Work with a teacher to represent sorted objects on a chart or graph.
- Work with a teacher to predict the results of a data collection.

First Grade

Measurement and Data

Measure lengths indirectly and by iterating length units.

- Compare and order three objects by length.
- Express the length of an object as a whole number of length units.
- Understand that length units must be the same size and have no gaps or overlaps.

Tell and write time.

- Tell and write time in hours and half-hours using analog and digital clocks.

Represent and interpret data.

- Organize, represent, and interpret data with up to three categories.
- Ask and answer questions such as the total number represented, how many in each category, and differences between categories.

---

*Although Common Core State Standards are not yet available for prekindergarten, Pre-K students may be expected to demonstrate some level of competency for these skills.

K.MD.A.1

K.MD.A.2

K.MD.B.3

K.MD.A.1

K.MD.A.2

K.MD.B.3

K.MD.A.1

K.MD.A.2

K.MD.B.3

K.G.A.1

Describe objects in the environment using names of shapes, and describe the relative positions of these objects using terms such as *above*, *below*, *beside*, *in front of*, *behind*, and *next to*.

K.G.A.2

Correctly name shapes regardless of their orientations or overall size.

K.G.A.3

Identify shapes as two-dimensional (lying in a plane, "flat" or three-dimensional "solid").

K.G.B.4

Analyze and compare two- and three-dimensional shapes, in different sizes and orientations, using informal language to describe their similarities, differences, parts (e.g., number of sides and vertices/"corners") and other attributes (e.g., having sides of equal length).

K.G.B.5

Model shapes in the world by building shapes from components (e.g., sticks and clay balls) and drawing shapes.

K.G.B.6

Compose simple shapes to form larger shapes. *For example, "Can you join these two triangles with full sides touching to make a rectangle?"*

_____

_____

_____

_____

_____

_____

_____

_____

_____

Prekindergarten*
Children should demonstrate increasing competency in the following, with guidance and support:
- Identify, describe, and construct different shapes including squares, circles, triangles, rectangles, hexagons, cubes, cones, cylinders, and spheres.
- Describe objects in the environment using names of shapes.
- Use positional words to identify positions of objects and people such as *above*, *below*, *behind*, and *under*.
- Identify shapes as two-dimensional (plane) or three-dimensional (solid).
- Compose larger shapes from simple shapes.
- Create a picture or design with different shapes.

First Grade
Geometry
Reason with shapes and their attributes.
- Distinguish between defining attributes and non-defining attributes.
- Build and draw shapes with defining attributes.
- Compose two-dimensional shapes (rectangles, squares, trapezoids, triangles, half circles, and quarter circles) or three-dimensional shapes (cubes, right rectangular prisms, right circular cones, and right circular cylinders) to create a composite shape, and compose new shapes from the composite shape.
- Partition circles and rectangles into two and four equal shares, using the words *halves*, *fourths*, and *quarters*, and the phrases *half of*, *fourth of*, and *quarter of* to describe the shares.
- Understand that decomposing a whole into equal shares creates smaller shares.

*Although Common Core State Standards are not yet available for prekindergarten, Pre-K students may be expected to demonstrate some level of competency for these skills.

K.G.A.1															
K.G.A.2															
K.G.A.3															
K.G.B.4															
K.G.B.5															
K.G.B.6															

K.G.A.1																				

K.G.A.1																				
K.G.A.2																				
K.G.A.3																				
K.G.B.4																				
K.G.B.5																				
K.G.B.6																				

44

Reading Standards for Literature

RL.K.1 With prompting and support, ask and answer questions about key details in a text.

RL.K.2 With prompting and support, retell familiar stories, including key details.

RL.K.3 With prompting and support, identify characters, settings, and major events in a story.

RL.K.4 Ask and answer questions about unknown words in a text.

RL.K.5 Recognize common types of texts (e.g., storybooks, poems).

RL.K.6 With prompting and support, name the author and illustrator of a story and define the role of each in telling the story.

RL.K.7 With prompting and support, describe the relationship between illustrations and the story in which they appear (e.g., what moment in a story an illustration depicts).

RL.K.8 (not applicable to literature)

RL.K.9 With prompting and support, compare and contrast the adventures and experiences of characters in familiar stories.

RL.K.10 Actively engage in group reading activities with purpose and understanding.

Standards Crosswalk

Prekindergarten*

Children should demonstrate increasing competency in the following, with prompting and support:

- Ask and answer questions about a story or poem that is read aloud.
- Retell main ideas from a story or poem that is read aloud.
- Ask and answer questions or act out characters and events from a story or poem that is read aloud.
- Show interest in learning new vocabulary.
- Recognize the difference between different types of text.
- Draw pictures to make connections to the text or to themselves.
- Make connections between a story or poem and their experiences.
- Compare and contrast two stories about the same topic.
- Describe the role of the author and the illustrator.
- Participate in group literacy activities with purpose and understanding.

First Grade

Reading: Literature

Key Ideas and Details

- Ask and answer questions about key details in a text.
- Use key details to retell stories.
- Understand the message or lesson of a story.
- Use key details to describe characters, settings, and major events in a story.

Craft and Structure

- Identify words and phrases that suggest feelings or appeal to the senses.
- Explain differences between fiction and nonfiction books.
- Identify who is telling the story at various points in a text.

Integration of Knowledge and Ideas

- Use illustrations and details in a story to describe its characters, setting, or events.
- Compare and contrast the adventures and experiences of characters in stories.

Range of Reading and Level of Text Complexity

- Read prose and poetry of appropriate complexity for grade 1.

*Although Common Core State Standards are not yet available for prekindergarten, Pre-K students may be expected to demonstrate some level of competency for these skills.

RL.K.1																				
RL.K.2																				
RL.K.3																				
RL.K.4																				
RL.K.5																				
RL.K.6																				
RL.K.7																				
RL.K.9																				
RL.K.10																				

48

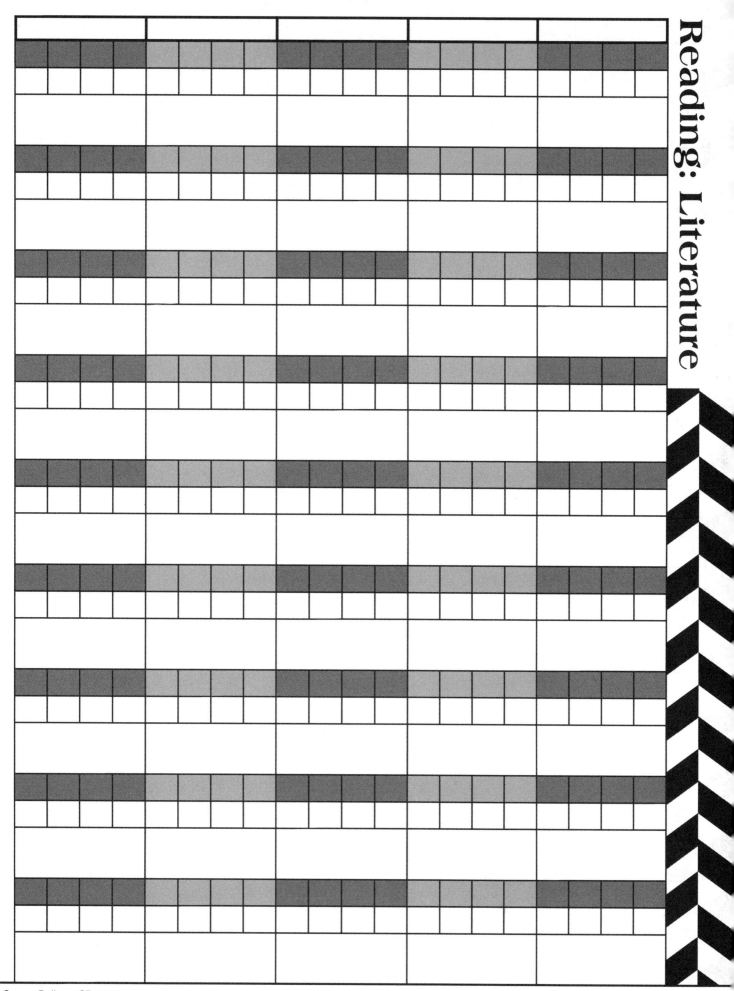

RL.K.1																				
RL.K.2																				
RL.K.3																				
RL.K.4																				
RL.K.5																				
RL.K.6																				
RL.K.7																				
RL.K.9																				
RL.K.10																				

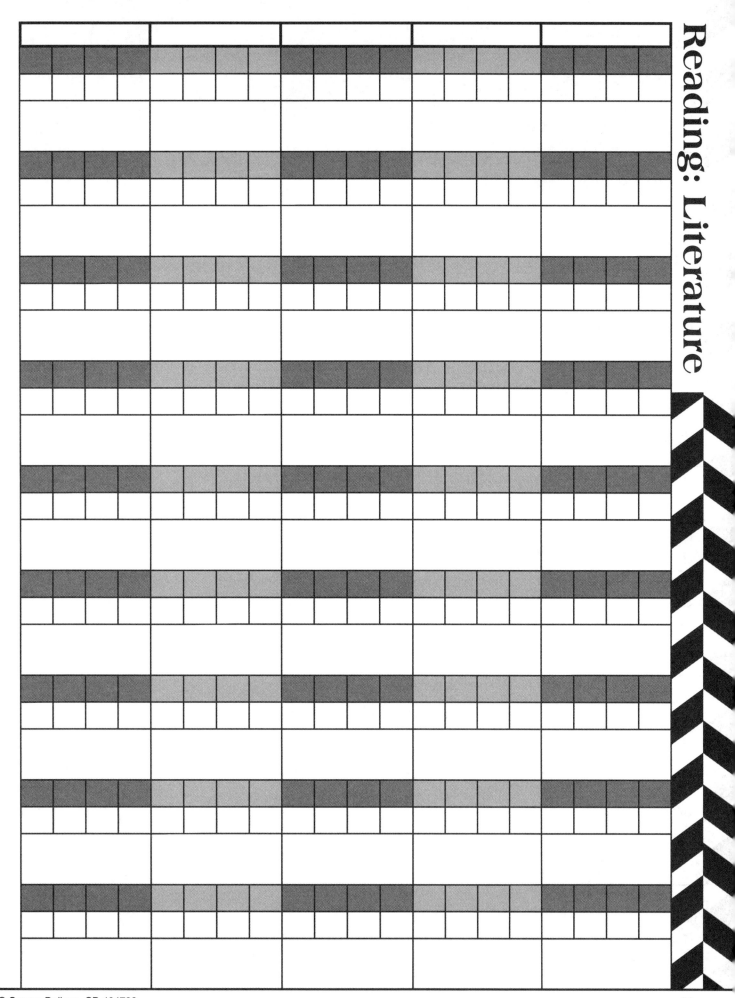

RL.K.1					
RL.K.2					
RL.K.3					
RL.K.4					
RL.K.5					
RL.K.6					
RL.K.7					
RL.K.9					
RL.K.10					

52

Reading Standards for Informational Text

RI.K.1	With prompting and support, ask and answer questions about key details in a text.
RI.K.2	With prompting and support, identify the main topic and retell key details of a text.
RI.K.3	With prompting and support, describe the connection between two individuals, events, ideas, or pieces of information in a text.
RI.K.4	With prompting and support, ask and answer questions about unknown words in a text.
RI.K.5	Identify the front cover, back cover, and title page of a book.
RI.K.6	Name the author and illustrator of a text and define the role of each in presenting the ideas or information in a text.
RI.K.7	With prompting and support, describe the relationship between illustrations and the text in which they appear (e.g., what person, place, thing, or idea in the text an illustration depicts).
RI.K.8	With prompting and support, identify the reasons an author gives to support points in a text.
RI.K.9	With prompting and support, identify basic similarities in and differences between two texts on the same topic (e.g., in illustrations, descriptions, or procedures).
RI.K.10	Actively engage in group reading activities with purpose and understanding.

Standards Crosswalk

Prekindergarten*

Children should demonstrate increasing competency in the following, with prompting and support:

- Ask and answer questions about informational text read aloud.
- Recall important facts after hearing a text read aloud.
- Act out concepts learned from informational text.
- Show interest in learning new vocabulary.
- Handle books correctly, identifying their front and back covers.
- Describe details from a photo or illustration.
- Describe the roles of the author and the illustrator.
- Participate in group reading activities with purpose and understanding.

First Grade

Reading: Informational Text

Key Ideas and Details

- Ask and answer questions about key details in a text.
- Identify the main topic and retell key details of a text.
- Connect two individuals, events, ideas, or pieces of information in a text.

Craft and Structure

- Ask and answer questions to help understand the meaning of words and phrases.
- Know and use text features (headings, tables of contents, glossaries, electronic menus, icons) to locate key facts or information in a text.
- Distinguish information provided by visual aids from information provided by the words in a text.

Integration of Knowledge and Ideas

- Use the illustrations and details in a text to describe its key ideas.
- Identify the reasons an author gives to support points in a text.
- Identify basic similarities or differences between two texts on the same topic.

Range of Reading and Level of Text Complexity

- Read informational texts that are appropriately complex for grade 1.

*Although Common Core State Standards are not yet available for prekindergarten, Pre-K students may be expected to demonstrate some level of competency for these skills.

RI.K.1																			
RI.K.2																			
RI.K.3																			
RI.K.4																			
RI.K.5																			
RI.K.6																			
RI.K.7																			
RI.K.8																			
RI.K.9																			
RI.K.10																			

RI.K.1																			
RI.K.2																			
RI.K.3																			
RI.K.4																			
RI.K.5																			
RI.K.6																			
RI.K.7																			
RI.K.8																			
RI.K.9																			
RI.K.10																			

58

RI.K.1					
RI.K.2					
RI.K.3					
RI.K.4					
RI.K.5					
RI.K.6					
RI.K.7					
RI.K.8					
RI.K.9					
RI.K.10					

Reading Standards: Foundational Skills

RF.K.1 Demonstrate understanding of the organization and basic features of print.
 RF.K.1a Follow words from left to right, top to bottom, and page by page.
 RF.K.1b Recognize that spoken words are represented in written language by specific sequences of letters.
 RF.K.1c Understand that words are separated by spaces in print.
 RF.K.1d Recognize and name all upper- and lowercase letters of the alphabet.

RF.K.2 Demonstrate understanding of spoken words, syllables, and sounds (phonemes).
 RF.K.2a Recognize and produce rhyming words.
 RF.K.2b Count, pronounce, blend, and segment syllables in spoken words.
 RF.K.2c Blend and segment onsets and rimes of single-syllable spoken words.
 RF.K.2d Isolate and pronounce the initial, medial vowel, and final sounds (phonemes) in three-phoneme
  (consonant-vowel-consonant, or CVC) words. (This does not include CVCs ending with /l/, /r/,
  or /x/.)
 RF.K.2e Add or substitute individual sounds (phonemes) in simple, one-syllable words to make new words.

RF.K.3 Know and apply grade-level phonics and word analysis skills in decoding words.
 RF.K.3a Demonstrate basic knowledge of one-to-one letter-sound correspondences by producing the
  primary sound or many of the most frequent sounds for each consonant.
 RF.K.3b Associate the long and short sounds with the common spellings (graphemes) for the five
  major vowels.
 RF.K.3c Read common high-frequency words by sight (e.g., *the, of, to, you, she, my, is, are, do, does*).
 RF.K.3d Distinguish between similarly spelled words by identifying the sounds of the letters that differ.

RF.K.4 Read emergent-reader texts with purpose and understanding.

_____

_____

_____

_____

_____

_____

_____

_____

_____

_____

_____

_____

_____

_____

Standards Crosswalk

Prekindergarten*
Children should demonstrate increasing competency in the following:
- Understand that print can be read and has meaning.
- Follow words left to right, top to bottom, and page by page.
- Recognize some lower- and uppercase letters.
- Recognize and match rhyming words.
- Show awareness of the relationship between sounds and letters.
- Identify the beginning sound of a spoken word.
- Generate a list of words with the same initial sound.
- Show one-to-one letter sound correspondence of some consonants.
- Recognize own name and some environmental print.
- Display beginning reading behaviors such as pretend reading.

First Grade
Reading: Foundational Skills
Print Concepts
- Recognize the unique first word, capitalization, and punctuation of a sentence.

Phonological Awareness
- Demonstrate understanding of spoken words, syllables, and phonemes.
- Distinguish long from short vowel sounds in spoken single-syllable words.
- Orally blend sounds, including consonant blends, in single-syllable words.
- Isolate and pronounce initial, medial vowel, and final sounds in spoken single-syllable words.
- Segment spoken single-syllable words into all individual sounds.

Phonics and Word Recognition
- Decode words using grade-level phonics and word analysis skills.
- Know the spelling and sounds of common consonant digraphs.
- Decode regularly spelled one-syllable words.
- Know final -e and other common vowel team long vowel sound patterns.
- Determine the number of syllables in a word by knowing that each syllable must have a vowel sound.
- Break words into known syllables to decode two-syllable words.
- Read words with inflectional endings.
- Recognize and read grade-appropriate irregularly spelled words.

Fluency
- Read with accuracy and fluency to support comprehension.
- Read grade-level text with purpose and understanding.
- Read grade-level text orally with accuracy, fluency, and expression.
- Use context and rereading to confirm or self-correct understanding of text.

_____

_____

_____

_____

_____

_____

_____

_____

_____

_____

*Although Common Core State Standards are not yet available for prekindergarten, Pre-K students may be expected to demonstrate some level of competency for these skills.

RF.K.1																			

RF.K.2																			

RF.K.3																			

RF.K.4																			

RF.K.1																			
RF.K.2																			
RF.K.3																			
RF.K.4																			

RF.K.1

RF.K.2

RF.K.3

RF.K.4

Writing

W.K.1	Use a combination of drawing, dictating, and writing to compose opinion pieces in which they tell a reader the topic or the name of the book they are writing about and state an opinion or preference about the topic or book (e.g., *My favorite book is...*).
W.K.2	Use a combination of drawing, dictating, and writing to compose informative/explanatory texts in which they name what they are writing about and supply some information about the topic.
W.K.3	Use a combination of drawing, dictating, and writing to narrate a single event or several loosely linked events, tell about the events in the order in which they occurred, and provide a reaction to what happened.
W.K.4	(begins in grade 3)
W.K.5	With guidance and support from adults, respond to questions and suggestions from peers and add details to strengthen writing as needed.
W.K.6	With guidance and support from adults, explore a variety of digital tools to produce and publish writing, including in collaboration with peers.
W.K.7	Participate in shared research and writing projects (e.g., explore a number of books by a favorite author and express opinions about them).
W.K.8	With guidance and support from adults, recall information from experiences or gather information from provided sources to answer a question.
W.K.9	(begins in grade 4)
W.K.10	(begins in grade 3)

70

Standards Crosswalk

Prekindergarten*

Children should demonstrate increasing competency in the following, with prompting and support:

- Use drawings, dictating, or writing to express an opinion about a book or topic.
- Use drawings, dictating, or writing to compose informative or explanatory text that supplies information about a topic.
- Use drawings, dictating, or writing to narrate an event and tell how they feel about it.
- Respond to questions and suggestions to make illustrations or writing clearer.
- Recall information from a previous experience to answer a question.
- Participate in shared writing and research projects.

First Grade

Writing

Text Types and Purposes

- Write an opinion piece on a topic or book, and provide a reason and a closing.
- Write informative/explanatory text in which they name a topic, give facts about the topic, and provide a closing.
- Write a narrative recounting two or more sequenced events that uses details, order words, and provides a closing.

Production and Distribution of Writing

With guidance and support:

- Focus on a topic, respond to feedback from peers, and add details to strengthen writing.
- Use a variety of digital tools to produce and publish writing, including in collaboration with peers.

Research to Build and Present Knowledge

- Participate in shared research and writing projects.
- With guidance and support, recall information or gather information to answer a question.

*Although Common Core State Standards are not yet available for prekindergarten, Pre-K students may be expected to demonstrate some level of competency for these skills.

W.K.1																			
W.K.2																			
W.K.3																			
W.K.5																			
W.K.6																			
W.K.7																			
W.K.8																			

W.K.1																				
W.K.2																				
W.K.3																				
W.K.5																				
W.K.6																				
W.K.7																				
W.K.8																				

W.K.1																				
W.K.2																				
W.K.3																				
W.K.5																				
W.K.6																				
W.K.7																				
W.K.8																				

Writing

Speaking and Listening Standards

SL.K.1 Participate in collaborative conversations with diverse partners about *kindergarten topics and texts* with peers and adults in small and larger groups.

    SL.K.1a Follow agreed-upon rules for discussions (e.g., listening to others and taking turns speaking about the topics and texts under discussion).

    SL.K.1b Continue a conversation through multiple exchanges.

SL.K.2 Confirm understanding of a text read aloud or information presented orally or through other media by asking and answering questions about key details and requesting clarification if something is not understood.

SL.K.3 Ask and answer questions in order to seek help, get information, or clarify something that is not understood.

SL.K.4 Describe familiar people, places, things, and events and, with prompting and support, provide additional detail.

SL.K.5 Add drawings or other visual displays to descriptions as desired to provide additional detail.

SL.K.6 Speak audibly and express thoughts, feelings, and ideas clearly.

_____

_____

_____

_____

_____

_____

_____

_____

Standards Crosswalk

Prekindergarten*

Children should demonstrate increasing competency in the following, with prompting and support:

- Interact in conversations with diverse partners during daily routines and play.
- Use appropriate methods of group conversation such as waiting their turn to speak.
- Continue a conversation through several exchanges.
- Recall information for short periods of time from information presented through a book, recording, or video, and retell the information.
- Ask and answer questions to clarify, seek help, or get information.
- Describe real or imagined personal experiences.
- Create visual displays to represent stories or experiences.
- Speak audibly and express thoughts, feelings, and ideas.

First Grade

Speaking and Listening

Comprehension and Collaboration

- Participate in group discussions about grade-appropriate topics and texts.
- Follow agreed upon discussion rules.
- Respond to remarks of others.
- Ask for clarification if needed.
- Ask and answer questions about key details in a text or other channels of information.
- Ask and answer questions about what a speaker says to better understand something.

Presentation of Knowledge and Ideas

- Use relevant details, ideas, and feelings to describe people, places, things, and events.
- Add visual displays to clarify descriptions when appropriate.
- Produce complete sentences when appropriate.

*Although Common Core State Standards are not yet available for prekindergarten, Pre-K students may be expected to demonstrate some level of competency for these skills.

SL.K.1					
SL.K.2					
SL.K.3					
SL.K.4					
SL.K.5					
SL.K.6					

80

SL.K.1																			
SL.K.2																			
SL.K.3																			
SL.K.4																			
SL.K.5																			
SL.K.6																			

SL.K.1																		
SL.K.2																		
SL.K.3																		
SL.K.4																		
SL.K.5																		
SL.K.6																		

Language

Demonstrate command of the conventions of standard English grammar and usage when writing or speaking.

L.K.1a Print many upper- and lowercase letters.

L.K.1b Use frequently occurring nouns and verbs.

L.K.1c Form regular plural nouns orally by adding /s/ or /es/ (e.g., *dog*, *dogs*; *wish*, *wishes*).

L.K.1d Understand and use question words (interrogatives) (e.g., *who*, *what*, *where*, *when*, *why*, *how*).

L.K.1e Use the most frequently occurring prepositions (e.g., *to*, *from*, *in*, *out*, *on*, *off*, *for*, *of*, *by*, *with*).

L.K.1f Produce and expand complete sentences in shared language activities.

Demonstrate command of the conventions of standard English capitalization, punctuation, and spelling when writing.

L.K.2a Capitalize the first word in a sentence and the pronoun *I*.

L.K.2b Recognize and name end punctuation.

L.K.2c Write a letter or letters for most consonant and short-vowel sounds (phonemes).

L.K.2d Spell simple words phonetically, drawing on knowledge of sound-letter relationships.

(begins in grade 2)

Determine or clarify the meaning of unknown and multiple-meaning words and phrases based on *kindergarten reading and content*.

L.K.4a Identify new meanings for familiar words and apply them accurately (e.g., knowing *duck* is a bird and learning the verb *to duck*).

L.K.4b Use the most frequently occurring inflections and affixes (e.g., *-ed*, *-s*, *re-*, *un-*, *pre-*, *-ful*, *-less*) as a clue to the meaning of an unknown word.

With guidance and support from adults, explore word relationships and nuances in word meanings.

L.K.5a Sort common objects into categories (e.g., shapes, foods) to gain a sense of the concepts the categories represent.

L.K.5b Demonstrate understanding of frequently occurring verbs and adjectives by relating them to their opposites (antonyms).

L.K.5c Identify real-life connections between words and their use (e.g., note places at school that are colorful).

L.K.5d Distinguish shades of meaning among verbs describing the same general action (e.g., *walk*, *march*, *strut*, *prance*) by acting out the meanings.

Use words and phrases acquired through conversations, reading and being read to, and responding to texts.

Standards Crosswalk

Prekindergarten*

Children should demonstrate increasing competency in the following:

- Use oral language in everyday activities.
- Print some upper- and lowercase letters.
- Speak in complete sentences.
- Understand and use a growing vocabulary.
- Understand sentences with past, future, and present verb tenses.
- Understand concepts by sorting common objects into categories.
- Apply words learned in classroom activities to real-world examples.
- Use words and phrases acquired through conversation, listening to books real aloud, activities, and play.

First Grade

Language

Conventions of Standard English

- Use conventions of standard English grammar and usage in writing or speaking.
- Print all upper- and lowercase letters.
- Use common, proper, and possessive nouns; use singular and plural nouns with subject-verb agreement; use personal, possessive, and indefinite pronouns; use verbs to convey a sense of past, present, and future; use frequently occurring adjectives, conjunctions, and prepositions; use determiners such as *a*, *the*, *this*, *that*.
- Write and expand complete simple and compound declarative, interrogative, imperative, and exclamatory sentences in response to prompts.
- Use correct capitalization, punctuation, and spelling when writing.
- Capitalize dates and names of people; use end punctuation for sentences; use commas in dates and to separate words in a series.
- Spell words with common spelling patterns and common irregular words; spell unfamiliar words phonetically.

Knowledge of Language (Begins in grade 2)

Vocabulary Acquisition and Use

- Use sentence-level context clues to the meaning of a word or phrase.
- Use frequently occurring affixes as a clue to the meaning of a word.
- Identify common root words and their inflectional forms.
- Understand word relationships and nuances in word meanings.
- Sort and define words by categories to demonstrate understanding of the concepts they represent.
- Identify real-life connections between words and their use.
- Distinguish shades of meaning among verbs and adjectives.
- Use learned words and phrases, including common conjunctions such as *because.*

---

*Although Common Core State Standards are not yet available for prekindergarten, Pre-K students may be expected to demonstrate some level of competency for these skills.

L.K.1

L.K.2

L.K.4

L.K.5

L.K.6

88

L.K.1					
L.K.2					
L.K.4					
L.K.5					
L.K.6					

90

L.K.1					
L.K.2					
L.K.4					
L.K.5					
L.K.6					

Name _____   **Date** _____

Standard _____

_____

_____

_____

_____

Notes